This book is for all of Bart's friends and family and is dedicated to my mom, dad and sister with whom I have learned the simple joy of family tradition; and to Chamnap Faby, my wonderful (and very talented!) graphic designer, who has become a part of Bart's family.

.

Composed in the United States of America
First Imprint 2010
Bart Celebrates Christmas ©
ISBN 978-1-935824-96-1
SAN:850-637X

Library of Congress Cataloging –in-Publication Data
Bart Celebrates Christmas is composed and written by Pam Choi
Summary: Loveable Bart the cat shares his excitement to have a tree in the house
[1.Cats-fiction. 2. Pets-fiction. 3. Family-fiction. 4. Home-fiction 5. Christmas-fiction]
I. Title II. Choi, Pam

Bart Celebrates
Christmas

by **Pam Choi**

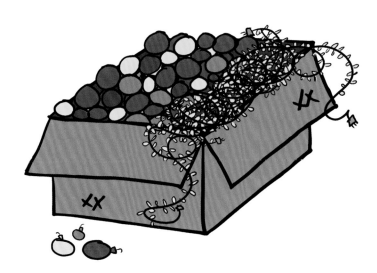

Hi! My name is Bart...

... Bart the Cat

I consider myself a cat of adventure and I have many tales to tell.

This tale is about celebrating Christmas with my family.

Christmas is coming and my Mom and Dad told me they were going to get a tree for the house.

A TREE in the HOUSE!

I can't wait to see this!

I waited by the door for the tree...

... And I waited.

When they finally brought the tree in the house I could not believe it.

The tree was sooo big!

And it smelled so nice!

I thought to myself, "Is this what a forest smells like?"

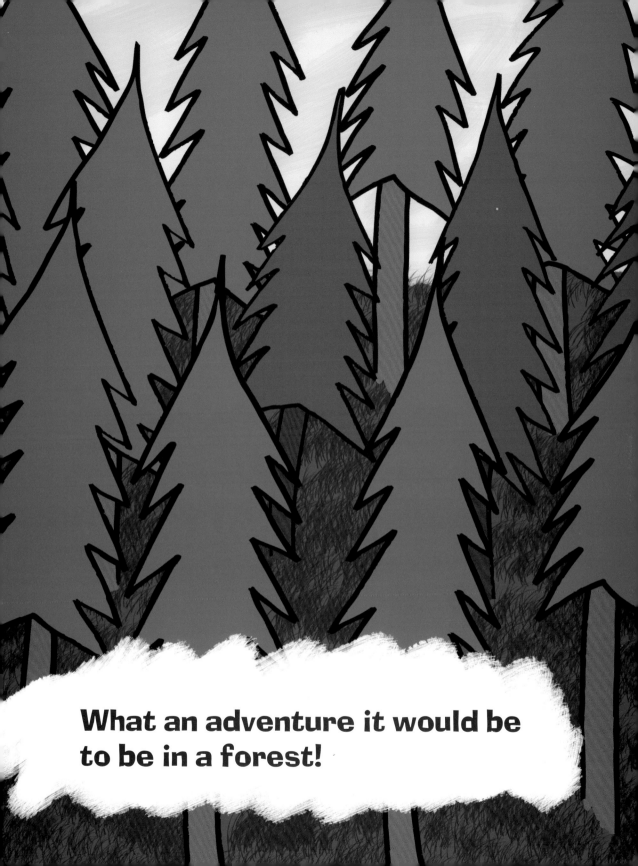

What an adventure it would be to be in a forest!

My Pop, (sometimes I call my Dad "Pop"), put the boxes with the Christmas tree lights and ornaments by the tree so they could start decorating.

I wanted to help, but Mom asked me to be a good boy and not to play with the decorations.

I always try to be a good boy for my Mom and my Pop.

Mom put Christmas music on the radio and started to sing along with the Christmas songs.

I love it when Mom sings.

Sometimes she picks me up and we dance around the room while she sings songs.

She says I am a good dancer!

Pop put lights all over the tree.

Then Mom put the pretty ornaments on the tree.

My favorite ornament is a bunny.
I think he looks like me.

Mom told me that when I was a little baby cat I climbed up into the Christmas tree and climbed out on a branch.

She said I looked like an ornament!

The last thing Dad put on the tree was an angel.

The angel watches over us from the top of the tree.

Mom says there are angels all over the world watching over us.

What an adventure it would be to be a Christmas Tree Angel!

When they finished decorating the tree, Dad turned off all of the lights in the room except the Christmas tree lights.

We all sat on the couch in the glow of the Christmas lights.

We looked at the tree and listened to the Christmas music.

Our Christmas tree was the most beautiful thing I had ever seen.

I was so happy to be with my family, waiting for Christmas and looking at the tree.

Guess what?

I hear Pop saying it's time for bed.

It's been a wonderful day and I am ready to go to sleep.

I can't wait until next time when I can tell you about more of my adventures.

Tonight I will dream about the
Christmas tree and the angels.

I hope you dream of beautiful trees
and angels too.

Until next time...

...Bart the Cat!